FOR BEGINNERS: METAVERSE

A COMPLETE GUIDE TO UNDERSTANDING THE NEW DIGITAL WORLD REVOLUTION. LEARN HOW TO INVEST IN BLOCKCHAIN GAMING, NFT, VIRTUAL LANDS, AND CRYPTO ART THROUGH BLOCKCHAIN GAMING

Thomas F. Escobar

Contents

Chapter One

Definition of Metaverse

The Metaverse is an online, 3D, and virtual realm that unites people from all walks of life. This proposal would enable various platforms to be linked together, similar to how the Internet provides access to many websites using a single browser now.

In essence, the Metaverse is a large infrastructure made up of linked virtual worlds that can be accessed via a common interface, the browser, which combines 2D and 3D features to create an immersive Internet. As a result, the Metaverse is not a single thing; rather, it is a collection of entities that reinforce one another through virtualization and 3D online technologies that will be integrated into our surroundings and become a part of our existence.

2 FOR BEGINNERS: METAVERSE

Snow Crash, a science fiction book by Neal Stephenson, introduced the notion. Despite the fact that the concept of a Metaverse was previously simply a work of fiction, it now seems like it may become a reality in the near future.

Each user will be able to control a character or avatar in the Metaverse, which will employ augmented reality. You could, for example, use an Oculus VR visor in your virtual workplace to attend a mixed reality conference, then complete your job and relax with a blockchain-based game before managing your bitcoin wallet and finances, all while staying in the Metaverse.

The ability to feel your presence with others within the same digital space is what separates the Metaverse from today's mobile internet. A three-dimensional digital sensory realm, as opposed to the flattened two-dimensional digital environment in which existing technologies and platforms operate. Users may freely roam about in this 3D digital area to enjoy and explore it in a more natural and tangible manner.

In existing virtual gaming environments, you may glimpse certain characteristics of the Metaverse. Social technologies in the workplace or games like Second Life and Fortnite. These apps aren't quite the Metaverse, but they're close. Currently, there is no Metaverse.

The Metaverse will merge economy, digital identities, decentralized government, and other applications, in addition to enabling games and social media. Even today, user creation, together with the ownership of assets and money, is assisting in the development of a distinct Metaverse. The blockchain has a lot of promise to fuel future technologies because of these qualities.

The Purpose of the Metaverse

Many huge IT corporations thought the metaverse would be the next digital revolution after the smartphone revolution. It has the potential to usher in a new economy as well as having significant societal implications.

Here are a few examples of software.

Shared work, video conferencing There is already a product from Facebook. Virtual guided tours of monuments are available for educational purposes.

We will be able to check whether a dress fits us better on eCommerce thanks to immersive and interactive buying.

Houses should be purchased from afar (already in the U.S., there are virtual reality services for buying and selling real estate).

Away from the crowds Virtual weddings and parties Pets that are only available online

A virtual reality sports experience

Chapter Two

Horizon Workrooms are combining Facebook with virtual reality.

Horizon Workrooms is a new virtual reality software from Facebook that can be used with Oculus Quest 2 VR viewers.

The goal presented by Facebook's titan, Mark Zuckerberg, is to enable people from all over the globe to interact, collaborate, and have meetings in a virtual workplace.

Horizon Workrooms symbolize the future of work, according to the Oculus blog of the same name, which can be viewed on Facebook. Apple's desktop application promises unprecedented levels of interaction and engagement for both Windows and Mac users. Users will be able to physically bring their desks, laptops, and other equipment into the virtual environment during meetings, for example, according to the business.

Horizon Workrooms will enable users to take notes and memoranda during meetings, as well as transfer files around in virtual reality and share documents, images, videos, and presentations on other people's displays. Of course, Facebook's objective isn't to build a new sophisticated video conferencing platform or to compete with the industry's other main competitors. The program wants to establish a new way of working online, according to spokespeople. Horizon Workrooms was established with the goal of making virtual work meetings more realistic. The availability of personalized avatars that mirror the user himself is one of the most engaging characteristics.

Furthermore, the Facebook app offers cutting-edge features including a new spatial sound system that changes your colleagues' audio and speech to be realistic based on their location in the virtual room.

Horizon Workrooms was conceived up and created by Facebook to be adaptable and inclusive: for example, the software does not exclude anybody who does not have virtual reality access. Horizon Workrooms enables one or more users to participate in a virtual meeting without wearing a virtual reality visor by using a traditional videoconference.

Investing in the Metaverse: What You Need to Know

Metaverse Economics

It is addressed how non-fungible tokens might assist in the development of civilizations in immersive virtual worlds. A normal day in the metaverse, a shared immersive virtual environment, may soon grow to resemble a typical day in our real-world reality, and vice versa. We will be able to visit retail malls, travel across town, meet pals in cafés, and exchange contacts in ways that seem stunningly genuine – and will be.

For many years, metaverses have existed as multiplayer online games, and they still exist today. Nonetheless, we may soon be approaching an era of immersive experiences that are practically indistinguishable from our real-world settings, encouraging new levels of involvement among gamers and non-gamers alike.

Two prototype next-generation metaverses, Decentraland and Somnium Space, already show the beginnings of complete civilization, with people populating the land, interacting socially, exchanging objects, and claiming ownership rights. A functional economy is required for every civilisation to function properly (physical or virtual). The authentication of digital items, such as a person's metaverse home, automobile, farm, books, clothing, and furniture, as well as the certification of digital identities, are critical in the metaverse. To prosper, it also needs the capacity to freely travel and trade among planets with varying laws and rules.

Non-fungible tokens, or digital records of digital ownership stored on a blockchain, will serve as the metaverse economy's basis due to their capacity to verify belongings, property, and even one's own identity. Because each NFT is secured by a cryptographic key that cannot be erased, duplicated, or destroyed, it enables the strong, decentralized verification - of one's virtual identity and digital assets – that is essential for a metaverse society to succeed and communicate with other metaverse societies.

The significance of NFTs may lie in the fact that they have enabled the emergence of something that resembles genuine human society in the metaverse, characterized by free markets (for goods, services, and ideas), independent ownership, and social contracts, in addition to the media attention generated by multi-million-dollar digital art sales.

In the brave new world of the twenty-first century, real estate development is a hot topic. People converse among fountains, browse at fancy boutiques, and jog along the beach in Decentraland.

Customers are drawn to high-stakes poker games by promenades and casino croupiers.

Due to the spontaneous growth of virtual real estate by individuals who have acquired property and constructed landscapes that have grabbed the imagination of other

Decentraland inhabitants, various relationships have been established.

While the experience is far from realistic (the makers of Decentraland argue that the planet is still in the "Iron Age"), it is entertaining. Regardless, even with these early versions, the potential is obvious and enticing. People in the metaverse, much as in real life, gravitate toward interesting regions. Furthermore, much like it would in a real-world destination like Paris or Beverly Hills, popularity naturally enhances the value of the virtual property.

Decentraland's and other metaverses' economies are built on the concept of land adjacency. All metaverse parcels are contiguous to each other and the rest of the metaverse in a fixed location - within specified geography. Supply is limited due to the limited amount of available land. Scarcity also permits property prices to rise and fall in accordance with global supply and demand norms.

As a consequence, the Decentraland manifesto claims that a framework is being created for "a social experience with an economy fueled by the current layers of land ownership and content distribution." The Decentraland vision is then carried out using this structure.

Property transfers are enabled through NFTs, which is what propels the metaverse forward. In most cases, these tokens provide indisputable proof of ownership that is more secure than a property title.

Anziani feels it is difficult to create metaverse property rights in the actual world because of the way smart contracts and NFTs are created. "You are aware that you own an item and that you may establish total ownership; you may then claim ownership rights in that virtual environment depending on its conditions and circumstances."

In The Metaverse, Real Estate

Despite the fact that the metaverse is still in its infancy, platforms like The Sandbox and Decentraland have started to offer digital real estate in non-fungible tokens (NFTs), a sort of blockchain currency capable of representing a broad variety of unique goods. When someone buys metaverse real estate, the platform's blockchain network validates the transaction and transfers ownership to the buyer.

After acquiring virtual real estate NFT, a virtual real estate NFT owner may rent out, sell, or even build a home on it. Atari, a Japanese video game company, has purchased 20 digital properties in Decentraland and launched its own crypto casino there. Using Atari's native ERC20-based Atari token, which is totally tax-free, gamblers may place bets and receive payouts in bitcoin. In addition, Atari has announced ambitions to build a virtual hotel complex in the United Kingdom in 2022.

In the metaverse, you may purchase real estate and other digital goods. Several metaverse platforms have set up marketplaces under the pretext of NFTs where users may buy and sell digital land and other metaverse assets.

This is how you do it.

In order to buy digital real estate in the metaverse, the user must first decide which platform he will use. There are various options, including Decentraland and The Sandbox. Do your homework before acquiring any metaverse real estate.

To begin, the user must create a digital cryptocurrency wallet, which is a computer software that connects to a blockchain network and stores cryptocurrency. The connected blockchain, which is the platform that powers the metaverse, must also be compatible with the wallet.

The consumer must then go to the marketplace of their chosen metaverse platform and use their digital wallet to connect with it. On the websites of metaverse platform providers, marketplaces are often seen.

Buying digital real estate seems to be quite comparable to purchasing real estate in the real world at this stage. Before making a decision, a buyer should examine the price, location, and future potential value of the digital land he is considering purchasing.

Once a buyer has found a plot of land, he must get the tokens or coins that were used to pay for it and deposit them in his digital wallet. Depending on whether metaverse platform is utilized, the kind of token or money necessary to execute the transaction will vary. To buy digital land in Decentraland, for example, purchasing MANA tokens would be necessary. To buy land in The Sandbox, he'll need SAND tokens, which he'll have to acquire.

If the buyer has already connected his digital wallet to the metaverse marketplace and funded it, all he needs to do now is bid on the land or buy it straight from the seller. The land will be removed from the user's digital wallet and replaced with an NFT equivalent. Purchases of non-transactional metaverse items, such as avatar clothing and accessories, follow the same approach.

In the Metaverse, Cryptocurrency

Fungible tokens, which are divisible and can be exchanged between participants in the metaverse, are used to power metaverse projects that operate on blockchain networks. These tokens may be exchanged for digital products like virtual land, avatar apparel, and virtual cash. They may also be traded for regular cash or other cryptocurrencies. Cryptocurrencies used in the metaverse, such as Bitcoin and Ethereum, allow its owners to vote on decisions made inside the network, such as where money should be invested or when new features should be provided first.

Theoretically, if the value of digital assets increases, so should the value of the tokens associated with those assets. Furthermore, many metaverse platforms, such as Decentraland, burn all MANA tokens used to buy digital assets, permanently removing them from circulation and increasing the value of the remaining tokens in circulation.

The following table lists the tokens in the metaverse in decreasing order of market capitalization (market cap). Because of the inherent risk of the options they provide, they should be considered a speculative investment. Never invest more money than you are willing to lose in a business endeavour.

At the time of writing, the market capitalization of Decentraland's MANA token was over $6 billion. The MANA token is used to power the Decentraland metaverse as well as to transact on the platform's marketplace.

In contrast to Decentraland's MANA token, which can be used to buy digital goods and services, the AXS token can only be used for governance. Members of the community who own AXS will be able to vote on suggested actions that would have an influence on the Axie Infinity ecosystem, such as how the community treasury's funds are used. Axie Infinity's marketplace will accept AXS tokens for rapid purchases of digital goods and services.

Players may communicate with one another in The Sandbox by using user-generated content. Similar to Roblox, The Sandbox is a game. In return for participating in alpha testing, individuals will get a SAND token from the Sandbox. SAND tokens may be bought on digital exchanges in addition to conventional marketplaces. SAND is a utility token that may also be used for staking and governance. Members of the Sandbox community who own sand may use it to purchase digital goods and services, vote on new initiatives inside the Sandbox, and stake their sand for further rewards. The Enjin Coin (ENJ) cryptocurrency is used by this blockchain gaming enterprise, which runs on the Ethereum network. Rather than a single metaverse product like The Sandbox or Axie Infinity, Enjin offers a network of servers and servers that connect gamers to a range of connected play-to-earn gaming experiences. Every NFT developed inside the Enjin ecosystem is "infused" with ENJ, the ecosystem's native token that offers real-world value for digital assets.

Chapter Three

NFT "Predecessor of the Metaverse": Virtual Real Estate

The internet's real estate NFT irreversibly affects our perceptions of digital goods. Every aspect of everyday life is migrating to the virtual domain as technology evolves with civilization. Work, education, and conferences, which were formerly conducted in physical locations, are increasingly moving to the digital domain. Using a tablet, smartphone, or computer, anybody, regardless of their background, may do things quickly and easily. In terms of convenience, though, the virtual real estate NFT mania has been the biggest surprise.

You've undoubtedly heard of non-fungible tokens (NFTs) and know what they are. You also learnt how nonlinear optical fibers (NFTs) changed the digital art scene in 2021 and became more popular. You may not be aware, however, that blockchain real estate is exclusively accessible in the digital environment and can only be acquired via cryptocurrency exchanges.

It doesn't end there: certain virtual real estate NFTs are connected to physical buildings as well. The design and construction of real-world buildings might be influenced by these digital constructions.

The purpose of this research is to look at the phenomenon of virtual real estate NFT and how it affects the sector. The study also shows how to benefit from it by building virtual real estate NFTs.

The Virtual Real Estate NFT Phenomenon's Emergence

According to rumors, an online auction in 2020 sold a digital artwork for more than $500,000 (USD). It was the world's first NFT digital house, and it was a watershed moment in NFT technological development. The craze for non-financial virtual real estate transactions began with this transaction (NFTs).

A property on the legendary Decentraland was sold for almost $300,000, according to the NFT monitoring website NonFungible.com. Sommium Space, another well-known game, revealed that a plot was sold for more than $500,000. Users may meet new people, participate in events, and do things they would normally do in real life in these digital environments (also known as metaverses).

There are numerous types of metaverses, and each one attracts a distinct audience. Shopping malls and museums are two famous examples of metaverses with extensive content.

These digital environments get the most traffic and have the most users.

NFT was a pioneer in the field of virtual real estate.

The pioneers of the current metaverse phenomenon are blockchain technology and cryptocurrency. It was in 2008 when the two ideas were first introduced to the public. Cryptocurrency is a kind of digital money that is stored on the blockchain, a public ledger. This website allows users to exchange fiat dollars for digital currency. Each cryptocurrency has its own exchange rate, which in terms of functionality is comparable to that of a traditional currency exchange.

As shown by the fact that blockchain technology and cryptocurrencies are extensively employed today. Some investors pointed out that this industry's adoption rate is much greater than when mobile devices were originally introduced in 2007. Blockchain technology is here to stay, as shown by the growing number of people who depend on Internet of Things (IoT)-enabled products. Many investors believe that the technology will continue to improve and gain general adoption in the near future.

The industry is seeing a surge of new digital advancements as a consequence of the growing use of blockchain technology. It's no surprise that virtual real estate is the next big thing in the digital world.

Chapter Four

Virtual As Well As Physical Real Estate

Users in virtual settings like Decentraland may take part in events just as they would in real life. Decorating their homes, going to events, meeting new friends, and so on are examples of their activities. Users build avatars that are exact replicas of themselves.

Virtual real estate investing employs an investment strategy that is recognizable to anybody who has studied real estate. In the real world, many property owners have a diverse portfolio of assets, and the same is true in the metaverse. Despite the fact that virtual real estate NFTs are a relatively new concept, their quick adoption has raised them to the status of an asset class akin to real estate.

At this time, the most in-demand metaverse properties are in cities. A metaverse with a lot of material attracts more people, increasing its value. In both the real and virtual worlds, the notion that metropolitan places are more costly than suburban ones prevails. As a consequence, virtual real estate developers pay special attention to these spots and try to recreate them in the virtual world.

The scarcity of resources is another aspect that links the two. A limited number of parcels are available for purchase in every metaverse. These are NFT-created digital land tracts. They are non-financial entities that trade in virtual real estate, and the most well-known ones fetch astronomical prices. Despite the huge demand for popular plots, there isn't enough supply to meet it. Mortgages and interest rates are even included in the price of certain residences. Virtual properties built for users may be rented out. Decentralized finance, or DeFi, is a term used in the metaverse to refer to the process of making financial decisions. This program is a blockchain-based financial application with an automated workflow. This strategy benefits customers since it helps them to make informed financial decisions while also safeguarding their accounts.

Advantageous characteristics of virtual real estate NFT

The reach of virtual real estate is a significant advantage over physical real estate. This is a big advantage for marketers and large organizations that want to reach a broader audience with their goods and services than they might otherwise.

IKEA Taiwan, for example, capitalized on the current digital furniture obsession by creating an in-game version of their catalogue. This technique built a link between the company's platform and store and the IKEA-themed islands. Because of the plan, the company's target demographic expanded. These customers are usually reluctant to purchase IKEA furniture in person, but they are eager to purchase IKEA digital furniture.

For those who benefit from NFT development in virtual real estate, it's a boon. The real estate industry's future is being driven by technological advances. Everyone understands that real estate is one of the world's oldest industries, and it is unlikely to go away very soon. There will always be a demand for real estate, which has been proven. Because we live in a technologically dependent society, investing in virtual real estate NFT development is a smart move. This strategy will help you adapt to and plan for a technologically advanced future.

What does the future hold for the Metaverse?

Corporations with substantial metaverse investments are spending millions of dollars to persuade customers that the metaverse's dawn has finally arrived. Will it usher in a new era of widespread adoption and barrier-free digital communication, or will it remain a niche product reserved for gamers and other future tech enthusiasts? The only way to know for sure is to wait and see. For the time being, retail investors who are interested in the metaverse should look into these platforms and consider the metaverse's future worth.

Investing in Cryptocurrency with Smart Strategies

A collection of strategies and pointers to help you get started investing in cryptocurrency.

We go over some basic investing strategies for Bitcoin and other cryptocurrencies. The investment strategies listed below are all viable options for the volatile cryptocurrency market.

TIP: These are completely legal and above-board white-hat trading and investing strategies. This isn't investment advice, but rather educational and informative content aimed at helping you understand the fundamentals.

Before you invest, there are a few things you should consider.

First and foremost, before investing in cryptocurrency, consider the following:

Make time to complete your assignments. Use exchanges and wallets you're familiar with (I recommend Binance, which is arguably the most beginner-friendly exchange/wallet). Concentrate on coins that you believe in and are willing to "bag hold" (I only recommend Bitcoin and Ethereum; alts are higher risk / higher potential reward). TIP: I recommend "diversification," but it may be risky for a new investor. When you've figured out what you're doing, diversify your portfolio.

Start with the safest options, such as Bitcoin (and to a lesser extent, Ethereum), then move on to the top alts, such as BNB, before moving down the list.

Learn about the history of the market. Cryptocurrency markets are open every day of the week, 24 hours a day. Early in the morning, when the volume is low, large price movements are common. Crypto can go up 400% one day and down 80% the next, and a coin can go months without doing anything... It'll be difficult to predict which of those events will happen next. If you come in during a period when things are going well, you might assume things will always be this way, but that has never been the case. BTC and alts are up and down on a regular basis. Occasionally, alts appear to be in control; at other times, everything is up and down, and so on. Of course, things won't always be up, but when they are, they won't be for long (and the mood could very well change while you are sleeping or out on the weekend on a Saturday night). Only research and/or experience can adequately prepare you for the various Bitcoin worlds that exist.

Recognize that the market is volatile, and that while investing in cryptocurrencies is legal, many of the risks you will be taking are significant... Some may even appear to be gambling (similar to penny stock investing; it's investing, but you must be willing to lose 80% to 100% of your money if you HODL).

Take it slow and easy. By keeping your investment manageable and gradually entering the market over time, you can relieve a lot of the stress of day-to-day life. Limiting your crypto investments to 1%–4% of your investable cash, with buy-ins no higher than 10% of that, is a reasonable strategy. Even better if you use stop losses to mitigate risk and technical analysis to help you time the markets.

Consider the market from a long-term standpoint. Try not to get too caught up in the present unless your strategy calls for it. Instead, pick a strategy and an investment, stick to it, and keep a long-term view of the market in mind. It's fine to change your strategy as you gain experience; just make sure you have a strategy and a goal in mind. You can invest, trade, or combine the two. If you're investing, limit your trading and avoid obsessing over the day's dollar values. Keep an eye on your dollar values if you're trading, and avoid HODLing during the peak.

Recognize and acknowledge your emotions. Emotions almost always lead to financial loss. The only time you get lucky and FOMO buy at the bottom or panic sell at the top is if you're lucky. Always rely on data, not your gut, heart, or anything else that is not based on data. FOMO (fear of missing out) should be avoided at all costs.

Start small and build from there. Begin with a small amount of money and gradually increase it once you've verified that everything is working properly. This guidance covers a variety of topics, including sending money between peers, testing a bot or TA approach, trading, and more.

Know the rules and ramifications of the tax code. There are a few rules to follow, as well as some complicated tax laws. It's not impossible if you plan ahead of time, but it's also not something you should overlook. As a general rule, anything that is controversial in everyday life (online gambling, buying things on the dark web, not paying your taxes, etc.) is suspect in the cryptosphere.

Observe the current pattern. If you can distinguish between a bull and a bear market, you'll have a much better chance of succeeding.

Cryptocurrency Investing: The Fundamentals

If you keep all of the above in mind and plan on strategically investing in or trading cryptocurrencies you like, have a firm grasp on the market's volatility history, and know which exchanges to use... Then choose one or two investment/trading strategies.

Here are a few general investing strategies that you might find useful.

Today, "just HODL" and go all-in (try to avoid this one)

Going all-in today and "just HODL" is the coolest thing to do. That method has the same problem as going to a roulette table and betting everything on black. While this is correct, the strategy is simplistic. If you miss the market's absolute bottom, you may find yourself with few options but to cut losses or wait.

Bottom line: Long-term investing is probably the best strategy on the planet... until it isn't. When it comes to investments, you should always have a plan in place. It's usually a good idea to sell or take profits when a bull market ends. Buy and hold is a viable option if you're looking for a long-term investment, and any price is usually acceptable. Nonetheless, there's a risk of going all in at the top and HODLing the rest of the way down with this one. That can be excruciatingly painful, so consider the alternatives.

Before HODLing, take a middle position.

This simple and conservative method relieves you of the daily price swings. You can either buy at regular intervals regardless of price or buy incrementally as the price falls over time. Market mistiming can be avoided by building a long position over months or even years. Meanwhile, you can take part or all of the gains as they appear (and then reinvest those later if and when you see more attractive prices). It's also likely that you'd prefer to transition out of roles in stages. You can reduce your risk while investing by gradually entering and exiting positions over time. For a volatile, high-risk, high-reward asset such as Bitcoin, this can be an excellent strategy. You may also avoid some of the issues that traders face when filing complex crypto taxes by paying the long-term capital gains tax rather than the short-term capital gains tax (which is about half as much).

To trade and buy low and sell high, you don't need to know much more than how to buy and sell cryptocurrency. Buy when you think prices are low, such as after a few days of declining prices, and sell when prices are higher. Set stop losses or "hold bags" if you make a mistake (basically reverting to a "build an average position and hold" method if you make a mistake). Technical analysis is required if you want to be a pro at this (TA). Support levels, moving averages, and other indicators can all be used to make buy and sell decisions with TA. TA can help you increase the profitability of your trades if done correctly, but if done incorrectly, it can psych you out. Keep an eye out for fees and portfolio erosion if you decide to trade.

Experienced traders can outperform HODLers in sideways markets, and they can even outperform them in down markets. Traders are likely to miss out on some spectacular and brief runs as they chase the final coin to the ground while missing the next one in line. If you don't have the time or attention to dedicate to the volatile crypto markets 24 hours a day, seven days a week, consider trading only a portion of your total investable cash.

It takes time and discipline to become a good crypto trader (super fun, though).

Bottom line: Trading is fun, and if you are skilled, disciplined, and knowledgeable about technical analysis, it can be the most profitable method. "Noobs" are more likely to get "rekt" trading for various complex reasons. Even though no one expects to outperform a HODLer by trading, the majority of people do (as far as my research suggests). It's okay to get a few bruises on the way to recovery, but don't delude yourself into thinking you've arrived when you haven't. Start with small buy-ins and don't trade too frequently because you're probably not an expert.

TIP: Crypto-to-crypto or crypto-to-crypto trading is possible. Crypto-to-crypto has the added advantage of keeping you in crypto while you try to increase your holdings in a specific coin. However, it is more difficult than it appears, and failing to do so can result in you missing out on runs... so keep that in mind.

Purchasing a Trading Bot is a great way to diversify your portfolio.

Trading bots are computer programs that manage your trades on your behalf. The main benefit is that it can execute your commands while you sleep. It takes away all of the anxiety that comes with going to bed. If you're going to trade, setting up and operating a bot is probably worth the time, effort, and money. You don't have to do anything; just let it place stop losses for you, or if you're comfortable with technical analysis, let it trade death crosses and golden crosses on 2hr+ candles (this strategy is common enough that you should be aware of it on any timeframe; if everyone automates it with no additional parameters... every cross will be even more eventful than it already is).

Finally, A trading bot may be too difficult for a novice trader who isn't also an amateur coder with some basic trading and TA knowledge (it's not a high bar, but there are a few hurdles and learning curves). After you've mastered the technique, it will relieve a lot of stress from your day. You might not be able to sell at 4 a.m. if the market is dropping. Your bot may not be sitting at your computer, ready to buy the Golden Cross that appears while you're at work, but it is... and it is making decisions based solely on facts. Your crypto-bot will be able to make rational decisions on your behalf if you disconnect your emotions.

Using a Trading Bot to diversify your portfolio is a fantastic way to do so. "Trading bot" is a misnomer. When using a trading bot, you do not need to trade actively. It can be used to begin a coin collection or to manage risk. You can use a bot to protect or grow your money by employing sensible low-risk/low-reward strategies. You may want to invest in Bitcoin, but that doesn't mean you want to wait for it to plummet by 80%. Your emotions might get in the way, but your bot won't, so tell it what you're looking for and walk away.

Start with this strategy if you're going to use a bot. It's a great option for intermediate investors who want to get into crypto but don't want to be a victim and HODL every coin they own no matter what the market conditions are.

Arbitrage: Did you know you can buy a coin on one exchange for a lower price and sell it on another for a higher price? This is referred to as performing exchange arbitrage (or simply "arbitrage"). Arbitrage can be extremely profitable, but you must act quickly to take advantage of it. You can use a bot, but you'll have to give it withdrawal authority, which is a pain.

Conclusion: Due to the time it takes to transport cryptos between exchanges, this is a deceptively risky maneuver full of traps. It is, however, very simple and profitable when everything is in order. It's not for beginners, but it's something to aim for in your toolbox.

Here's a tip: if you already own the coin you're trading into and out of on both exchanges, you can buy and sell right away (rather than buying, sending, waiting, and selling).

Combine the above ideas: A combination of the above can be used to stay safe while learning about and enjoying the benefits of bitcoin. You could, for example, run one instance of your bot in invest mode and another in trading mode, trade a little manually, and keep the rest of your funds in a safe offline wallet. Perhaps your pocketbook, on the other hand, outweighs all of your other good intentions, and your bots shield you from emotional trading? The problem is that if one thing performs exceptionally well while the others do not, you now know what type of investor/trader you should be.

Bottom line: This is challenging because it necessitates learning and applying multiple solutions. On the other hand, for the vast majority of people, this should and would be the ultimate goal. So why not use them in tandem, picking the best tool for the job if you know how to use each one well enough?

You should, however, refine your own personal style. Similarly, I prefer to use small buy-ins to stop and ladder into and out of currencies, always keeping a portion of my money in cash and the rest in crypto, but I can't tell you how to play your hand. I'm trying to provide broad strategies rather than specifics here.

What You Should Know About Altcoin Investing

Before jumping, take a deep breath.

You can't enter any trade or investment arena, whether it's stocks or altcoins, without first learning about the market and the currencies you're interested in. Crypto markets are more volatile than traditional stock markets, and they deal in pegged financial assets and operate 24 hours a day, seven days a week, mediated by regulatory organizations like the SEBI in India. As a result, you should be aware that cryptocurrency markets are prone to wild swings in price. Keep track of the market's history or the performance of a specific cryptocurrency, investor sentiment, current developments in the crypto ecosystem, bearish or bullish market patterns, and other factors to better understand the situation.

You don't have to empty your altcoin wallet every time the value of your coin rises or falls. Instead, go with the currencies you trust, read their whitepaper, look at their team and roadmap, and examine the technology they employ to boost your confidence.

Following that, having a well-defined investment strategy with a clear goal will assist you in getting through even the most trying times. Finally, think about how long you want to hold the money in your hands: minutes, hours, days, months, or even years. You can also choose to day trade or 'bag hold' altcoins for the long term.

Use a reputable cryptocurrency exchange to trade and deal in altcoins. WazirX, India's most well-known cryptocurrency exchange, for example, enables you to trade safely, quickly, and easily.

Do not place all of your eggs in one basket.

The cryptosphere is a volatile environment in which events such as a minor technical team spat in Tezos or Musk shouting 'DOGE, DOGE, BABY DOGE' on Twitter can either shatter or build markets. As a result, it would be unwise to invest in a single currency. Rather, diversify your portfolio by investing in a number of alternative coins. The top ten cryptocurrencies by market capitalization, excluding Bitcoin, such as Dash, ETH, XRP, Litecoin, Cardano, and others, would be a safe bet for newcomers.

Bonus altcoin investment tip: Invest in cryptocurrencies that have yet to reach their full growth potential to see your money grow several times over time as the altcoin becomes more popular.

Place Your Trust In The Fundamentals

Unlike traditional equities, altcoins are far more than just trading assets. They each have a specific set of goals in mind. Smart contract platforms like Ethereum or NEO, or decentralized storage networks Filecoin or Storj, for example, aid in the mediation of currency prices, the acceleration of payment processes, and the strengthening of a platform's transparency and accountability. Use this two-pronged approach to evaluating the coin's fundamentals, rather than relying on public opinion:

Assess the concept's viability, practical use, and scope in order to determine the altcoin's lifespan.

Examine the scope and impact of the company's upcoming partnerships and releases on the market.

To reduce risk, diversify your altcoin portfolio within the category rather than investing in coins from different 'categories.'

Focus on the technical rather than the emotional.

FOMO, or any gut, liver, or heart emotion, isn't backed up by scientific evidence. Learning a few technical analysis nuances, on the other hand, can help you multiply your crypto investments. Simply determine whether the price is rising or falling, fluctuating or remaining constant, and adjust your investment strategy accordingly. If you know the altcoin's 50-day SMA (Simple Moving Average), you can spot positive price swings once the altcoin's price begins to move above its SMA. The price of an altcoin's ATH (All-Time High) is another useful technical indicator. You can calculate how much of the altcoin's ATH value corresponds to its current price. You'll be able to make better trading decisions if you study these signs on a regular basis prior to trading.

Is it better to stake, mine, or hold on to my money?

There are a variety of ways to grow your crypto investments depending on the altcoin you invested in:

Holding cryptocurrency is the safest, easiest, and fastest way to generate passive income from your assets. To invest in altcoins, you only need a safe crypto wallet and a reputable exchange. You can also buy cryptocurrencies in small amounts and gradually increase your holdings.

Staking is a way to earn passive income from your cryptocurrency investments by freezing or staking them on a network and receiving interest.

Mining altcoins can also help you earn monthly dividends. Individuals interested in earning rewards through mining should consider cloud mining or joining a mining pool, as solo mining, particularly in the case of Bitcoin, is expensive and time-consuming.

Chapter Five

Cryptocurrency Investments: How to Keep Them Safe

To hedge your crypto assets, you'll need to play smart with diversification. So, what's the most effective way to go about it? Consider diversifying your assets beyond cryptos, such as stocks, gold, and other traditional instruments, to build a portfolio that spans markets. The high correlation of the crypto market can be overcome by having a portfolio that includes both equities and cryptos. Simply put, an upward trend in Bitcoin, which accounts for 45 percent of the crypto market, always leads to an upward trend in the rest of the market, and vice versa. As a result, in the event of a market crash, there are no safe crypto assets on which you can rely. It's no surprise, then, that major investment funds are now attempting to combine the two.

Begin with a small investment and work your way up to liquidity.

Do some practice trading before going all-in on the crypto market. Start small and gradually expand your portfolio over time. Once you've realized you're on the right track, there's no going back. Trading regularly is another simple way to keep your funds moving and multiplying.

Liquidity is critical for keeping cryptocurrency investments safe and fluid. Altcoins with low trading volumes are often preferred by investors. This choice could prove to be costly. Altcoin prices may rise and fall, but you cannot profit from them by selling them. Due to a lack of liquidity, even if you can sell a large number of coins, prices may fall. So, what's the best way to keep yourself safe? Cryptocurrencies with a low volume of transactions should be avoided at all costs!

Metaverse's Benefits and Applicability

The Metaverse refers to online spaces where humans can connect in a more engaging and immersive way, as opposed to our current modes of communication. A good example of this is virtual reality (VR) headsets. The Metaverse is most often associated with multiplayer online gaming, but it can now also include video conferencing, social media, and live streaming. As this realm expands, so will the potential for personal identity, content creation, and even virtual economies. As major players in the digital sector continue to invest in the Metaverse's future, the pessimism surrounding its utility for commercial enterprises is starting to fade. Despite

Facebook's recent name change, many questions about the Metaverse's potential business benefits remain unanswered. Enterprise companies are more interested in the technology's potential to fundamentally change how they interact with their customers.

Benefits of a Metaverse Owned by a Corporation

In the metaverse, land, buildings, avatars, and even names can be purchased and sold, with bitcoin being the most common method of payment. In these settings, people can go for walks with their friends, visit buildings, buy goods and services, and attend events. The term refers to a wide range of virtual worlds, including business applications, games, and social networking sites. Many of the new platforms are based on blockchain technology and use cryptocurrencies and non-fungible tokens (NFTs) to enable the creation, ownership, and commercialization of a new kind of decentralized digital asset.

What role does the Metaverse play in the enterprise?

It's understandable to wonder about the Metaverse's utility. The Metaverse can assist enterprise businesses in three ways:

Giving people new ways to interact with businesses and their products.

promoting the acceptance of new currencies in the mainstream on a large scale Developing cutting-edge communication tools to aid collaboration among employees

It's critical to have a discussion about each point and to properly assess their value for business.

Relationships with Customers and Companies

The creation of new spaces for businesses to market their services is the Metaverse's first, and most likely, frontier. The most spectacular example of this is the Sotheby's Metaverse. Anyone can look at and buy NFT artworks on this online marketplace. Corporate interest in the Metaverse has always been piqued. Two popular online games, Roblox and Fortnite, are evolving from video games to full-fledged virtual worlds. Dave Baszucki, the game's co-founder and CEO, believes it could be the next step in professional communication. All of the practical benefits that the Metaverse can provide for corporate enterprises will most likely be directed to online markets. They may, however, be difficult to put into practice right away. Finally, small and medium-sized businesses must consider their clientele. If you work in IT and believe that some of your customers are already aware of these concepts, thinking about how to establish a Metaverse presence could be a good way to prepare for the future.

Currency Innovation

Due to the emergence of blockchain-based cryptocurrencies and the fact that most Metaverse platforms run on blockchain technology, enterprise businesses can now sell their services on a completely new marketplace. While cryptocurrency is undeniably becoming a global staple, the Metaverse embraces it even more. In addition to its own Metaverse, Sotheby's has opened an NFT gallery in Decentraland. This implies that decisions are made from the bottom up rather than the top down. Users in Decentraland, on the other hand, are free to make their own decisions. MANA, Decentraland's official currency, is a crucial component of the decentralized experience. Decentraland's Metaverse is an excellent example of how new currencies and companies can emerge. More than $900,000 in transactions have been completed using MANA. Users can use their MANA to purchase NFTs and virtual properties in this Metaverse, or they can gamble more in virtual casinos. This type of example aids in the integration of real-world business operations with the Metaverse. Businesses today should start thinking about how they can convert their business models to the Metaverse if Gucci and Sotheby's can do it successfully. This trend will only continue to grow as cryptocurrency becomes more mainstream.

Collaboration Among Enterprise Employees

Although the Metaverse's financial benefits are critical for enterprise businesses, it also allows for new types of collaboration. Collaboration via Zoom is convenient, but as we learned during the pandemic, it can also be restrictive. The Metaverse can maintain the convenience of video conferencing while simulating the efficacy of real meetings by establishing digital conference rooms. Facebook and Zoom are two companies that are pioneering the use of the Metaverse to facilitate employee collaboration. Both companies have recently announced new technologies aimed at fostering a more genuine hybrid workplace culture. Horizon Workrooms can be downloaded by anyone with an Oculus VR headset. Workrooms allow users to share screens, write and draw on a shared whiteboard, and use spatial audio to make conversations feel more real. Zoom Meetings and Zoom Whiteboard are both being integrated into workrooms.

Metaverse's Potential Applications

As previously stated, today's businesses have every right to be wary of the Metaverse and what it might entail for their operations. Although some of the advantages may appear to be too high-level and abstract to implement right away, highly successful enterprise firms are investing in the future to reap the benefits that will inevitably follow. There are currently examples of the Metaverse actively assisting enterprise businesses until that time comes. Virtual reality gaming, digital art exhibits and marketplaces, as well as employee virtual collaboration centers, are all examples. These existing models should be studied by enterprise firms to gain a better understanding of the Metaverse, blockchain technologies, and how transactions could be conducted in an online environment. Below is a list of some of the Metaverse's most important business applications.

E-Commerce

This translates to significant cost savings as well as a smaller carbon footprint. The Metaverse takes things a step further by introducing a completely new revenue stream for digital goods. As a result, increased sales and the sale of digital assets in the Metaverse can benefit fashion, furniture, and other businesses.

Legal

The Metaverse as a concept, in general, has the potential to have a far more profound and important impact on how businesses are conducted. While major customer meetings are frequently held in person, you can imagine that this will become obsolete as the Metaverse becomes more widely accepted.

HR

Companies like Boeing and Hewlett Packard, which deal with complex machinery assembly and would otherwise need a lot of training and resources, are now using virtual reality and augmented reality to overlay instructions in a real-world environment and give someone a step-by-step playbook on how to put together a jet engine.

Sales/Marketing

You will be able to connect with the client in a way that you would not be able to if you flew to their office. They're doing it from the comfort of their own home now that they've put on the headset. In a way that no other salesperson does, team managers spend time with them. Kyle Dulay, co-founder of CollabstrVentures Inc., a Vancouver company that connects influencers with clients, believes the Metaverse will change the way businesses spend marketing dollars. As a result, instead of being centered on platforms, advertising spending may become more dispersed among independents.

Finance without a central bank

Cryptocurrencies and non-fungible tokens (NFTs), which are both supported by blockchain for security and validity, have grown in popularity. As the Metaverse grows in popularity, users will be able to explore virtual worlds, interact with others, and make online purchases using crypto and NFTs. Lending and trading of such assets is expected to expand in these virtual worlds as well. You've probably heard how Beeple's Christie's auction brought NFTs into the mainstream in 2021. Now, the first interactive digital art galleries are appearing, allowing NFT avatars to shop for art anonymously. The Metaverse is also preparing the gaming industry for non-fungible tokens and crypto assets.

Education

Metaverse's advantages are spreading to education, where a promising new technology may improve active class participation. 3D environments or virtual reality headsets can be used to create virtual spaces. As in games like Minecraft and Fortnite, where people can create their own virtual worlds, Metaverse's shared virtual space is currently regarded as a promising new platform for the future of education and learning. As a result of the pandemic, online education as a digital mode of teaching and learning has exploded. Metaverse has the ability to combine technology to help accelerate online delivery through creative and innovative solutions, propelling digitized education to new heights.

Adoption of the Metaverse by Enterprise Businesses: Risks

The Metaverse poses two major threats to enterprise businesses. The first is that, like many other blockchain technologies, the Metaverse appears to have an extremely bleak future. The Metaverse's longevity has been questioned due to the volatility of Bitcoin. Major corporations such as Facebook, Adobe, Nvidia, and BMW, on the other hand, are investing in its future, indicating that the Metaverse is gaining traction among the general public. It took a long time, but the Metaverse has gained mainstream acceptance in comparison to cryptocurrency. The threat of cyber-attacks is the second issue facing Metaverse's future. However, as the Metaverse gains acceptance, data use ethics and cybersecurity regulations will inevitably be imposed to address all of the Metaverse's concerns. Enterprise businesses, on the other hand, should keep an eye on any risks associated with the Metaverse and other blockchain technologies like crypto.

A Summary of Web 3.0

Even though Web 3.0 is still in its infancy, everyone from Elon Musk to Jack Dorsey is excited about it. We'll discuss how the new internet avatar will appear, as well as the advantages and pitfalls to avoid as a result of the technological transformation. Web 3.0, also known as the third version of the internet, is expected to revolutionize the way we browse, socialize, and shop online. Web 3.0 will increase customization, communal ownership, and content sharing, whereas Web 2.0 will boost communication and online interaction. The new version of the internet will make use of blockchain, the technology that underpins bitcoin and the other forms of cryptocurrencies, allowing decentralized networks to maintain the internet. As a result, website proprietors will no longer be reliant on corporate-owned servers.

According to a New York Times story, investors have already put $27 billion into Web 3.0 as the "future of the internet." However, there are always two sides to every coin, and while Web 3.0 has benefits, it also has drawbacks. Although Web 3.0 is still in its infancy, experts have developed a list of the advantages and disadvantages of future internet iteration. All of these advantages and disadvantages, on the other hand, are based on current facts. The final version of Web 3.0 is still in the works, and it may differ drastically from the current version. It's only a matter of waiting till that time comes.

Significance of Web 3.0

In a nutshell, the third Web iteration aims to provide users more control over web content. You won't need different accounts for each social site with Web 3.0; instead, you'll be able to roam across platforms, search for information, and even shop with just one. The next internet revolution is coming, and it will give users more control over their digital information.

Web 3.0 intends to eliminate any big intermediaries, such as centralized governing bodies or repositories and will be built on the blockchain technology supporting bitcoin and other cryptocurrencies. Simply put, Web 3.0 eliminates the need for multiple social media accounts. You could easily travel between multiple social media sites, search the internet for information, and even shop with only one account.

The 1.0 Web, or the first phase of the World Wide Web, began in the 1990s when the dot-com boom enabled simple access to information. On the other side, the information was jumbled and difficult to navigate. Google and MSN introduced the 2.0 Web in the late 1990s, bringing order to chaos by categorizing and logically displaying information. They aided in the ranking of search results depending on popularity. It became easier to share knowledge with others via the internet at the start of this period. This, on the other hand, led to a continuous transfer of\s

power to a few large corporations.

Content producers are proposing Web 3.0 as the internet's next version for reclaiming control. New search engines and social networks will have access to the internet, and content management will no longer be confined to a few corporations. Web 3.0 addresses connection, content relevancy, content outreach, and performance, while Web 2.0 addresses communication and online engagement. Following decades of focusing on the aesthetics of websites and online pages, work on expanding 'back end' capabilities has started. The user experience was the motivating element behind this advancement. The scope of Web 3.0 is rather broad.

Web 3.0 and Cryptocurrencies: What Does It Mean?

Web 3.0 aspires to make the internet a more "democratic" space, similar to blockchain technology. To incorporate decentralized applications (dApps) into the ecosystem, leading crypto players are using the blockchain's smart contract capabilities. DApps are computer apps that operate on a blockchain network of computers rather than on a single machine. Smart contracts and decentralized apps (dApps) will help automate activities in order to make the internet more democratic.

The most extensively used 3.0 Web blockchain, according to sources, is Ethereum. As a consequence, ether will get more attention. Helium, Polkadot, and Kusama are just a few of the crypto initiatives that have tried to improve the Web3 experience. Web3 will also integrate nicely with the metaverse, making it easier to acquire and trade non-fungible tokens (NFTs), which are used to indicate ownership of virtual goods and are represented by cryptocurrencies.

Web 3.0 Advantages

The following are some of the possible benefits of Web 3.0:

Reliability

Producers and consumers will have more alternatives with Web 3.0. Web 3.0 will use decentralized networks to guarantee that consumers retain control over their online data at all times. The next generation of the internet is predicted to be more trustworthy due to its decentralized design, which decreases the possibility of a single-point failure.

For Everyone and Anything: Web 3.0 does not need the control of a single organization. Larger businesses may not have total control over the internet. Decentralized apps, or dApps, can't be censored or limited in any way as a consequence.

The trend of personalizing the internet is growing.

Online 3.0 will be able to recognize your preferences, enabling you to radically personalize your web surfing experience. This will also make your online surfing more productive.

Sellers Will Benefit From Web 3.0.

Sellers can understand your buying needs and offer items and services that you are interested in acquiring with the help of Web 3.0's artificial intelligence. As a consequence, you'll see more relevant and higher-quality adverts that are more likely to be valuable to you.

Services that aren't harmed

Because all data would be kept on dispersed nodes as a consequence of decentralization, users will not have to worry about their accounts being terminated or services being interrupted for technical or other reasons.

Web 3.0's Cons

Fears about ownership

Former Twitter CEO Jack Dorsey claims that, contrary to common perception, ordinary people will not own Web

3.0 enterprises. It will be owned by investors and venture capitalists. This implies command and control might stay in one place.

Regulating is challenging.

Decentralization, according to some observers, will make it more difficult to oversee and regulate Web 3.0. This might increase cybercrime and online abuse, among other things.

Better Processors Are Necessary for Web 3.0.

With older devices, Web 3.0 will be incompatible. As a consequence, you'll need a device with above-average hardware to utilize the future version of the internet.

Existing webmasters will be forced to upgrade their sites.

As websites and applications that use Web 3.0 become more popular, existing businesses will be compelled to upgrade their digital services to avoid losing market share. Web 3.0 is a broad and interconnected network that allows for quicker access to personal and public information. The semantic network makes it simple for everyone to access your online public and private information, which is one of its advantages.

Metaverse of NFTs

Non-fungible tokens, or NFTs, are a kind of cryptocurrency. Fungibility refers to the ability to be replaced by something of equivalent value or usefulness. When anything is stated as non-fungible, it means that it has unique qualities that cannot be substituted or swapped with anything else.

A $1,000 bill, for example, may be exchanged for two $500 bills or five $200 bills without losing its value. When a $1000 bill is non-fungible, it has a one-of-a-kind characteristic that precludes it from being traded with other currencies.

Non-fungible materials include heirlooms and famous heirlooms. Textile items, jewelry, and sculptures are regularly employed. They cannot be replaced by another of the same sort since it is the original. Only photographs or reproductions of it are possible. Its ownership may also be handed down down the generations by inheritance or large payments to the owners.

In the virtual sense, a non-fungible token is a one-of-a-kind, non-transferable data unit kept in the form of a digital ledger. As one-of-a-kind items, NFTs may be connected to readily replaceable goods such as photos, videos, and sounds. Blockchain technology has the potential to provide public proof of ownership for the NFT. Each has a digital signature that prohibits NFTs from being swapped out.

Virtual Lives and NFTs

The vast majority of people can attest to having downloaded or streamed photographs, music, and films from the internet on their phones. Digital data, as is generally known, may be duplicated forever on phones, hard drives, and other auxiliary storage devices with little or no credit given to the owner, allowing for digital plagiarism.

Social media dominates our virtual life at the moment. Facebook, Instagram, and Twitter, among other prominent social media sites, help us to create a version of ourselves that we want to share with the rest of the world. This is why some people have many accounts on a same app, each for a different reason.

NFTs are sometimes known as "digital tokens." Ownership certificates for virtual or tangible objects are analogous to digital tokens. A shared ledger known as the blockchain is used to keep track of ownership, much like crypto-currency.

At any one moment, only one NFT may be owned by a single individual. NFTs may incorporate smart contracts to decide how future revenues are dispersed. The records can't be forged since the ledger is kept by hundreds of millions of computers all around the globe. Non-fungible assets may be purchased and sold in a normal market in a similar way to fungible commodities and services. It entails paying money to give another person ownership of a digital object. The NFT includes a digital file as well as physical object that may be duplicated indefinitely.

NFTs, on the other hand, are designed to provide the owner something that can't be replicated: ownership of the work. It allows the client to boast about the product.

Chapter Six

The Metaverse's Key is NFT Technology

NFT technology relies on blockchains as its base. Blockchains are a kind of data storage that makes modifying, hacking, or scamming the system very difficult or impossible. They're distributed public ledgers that track transactions.

With an identifying code and information, each NFT is uniquely identifiable and preserved on the blockchain. In this case, "metadata" refers to information that describes the NFT and is kept alongside it.

The Ethereum platform is heavily reliant on NFTs. Ethereum, like bitcoin and dogecoin, is a digital currency. Nonetheless, its blockchain allows for the usage and selling of NFTs, which include additional storage data that allows them to operate differently than ethereum. It's important to note that various blockchains may employ NFT in a number of ways.

NFTs use the same blockchain technology as cryptocurrencies, but they are not a payment method. Cryptocurrencies are fungible, but non-fungible tokens are not. An NFT will never be valued the same as another NFT, but a dogecoin will always be worth the same as another dogecoin.

It's possible that importing NFTs into the metaverse represents the metaverse's revenue model. It's what propels it forward. When the metaverse is widely accepted, it will become a tremendous economic force that will profoundly impact people's lives in the following years.

In recent weeks, the price of the metaverse NFT index has soared. By giving avatars or digital items a specific identity, the metaverse connects the digital and physical worlds. People's social media accounts have been hacked and used for evil reasons in the recent past.

Using the metaverse for sociability, commerce, entertainment, and other purposes could lead to shady characters gaining access to other people's accounts for personal gain. Incorporating NFTs into the metaverse is critical.

What does all of this mean for the Metaverse?

Accounts will become more customized, enabling you to communicate with the real individual instead of a lookalike. The things are authentic since they are tagged with NFTs. Maintaining market stability and scarcity might help sellers boost their sales. NFTs in the Metaverse may even be included in inherited wills, according to some.

The promise of the metaverse is ascribed to the freedom it allows; anybody in the metaverse may construct, purchase, and view NFTs in order to acquire virtual real estate, join social networks, establish virtual identities, and play games, among other things.

With corporations and people alike able to connect into metaverse frameworks, a wide variety of options for monetizing real-world and digital assets opens up.

NFTs' Metaverse Functions

The virtual world's future is in the metaverse. Many items would migrate from the conventional market to the metaverse if the metaverse took control, such as entertainment, socializing, buying, and selling. NFTs may be displayed and utilized in a variety of ways throughout the metaverse.

For the economy: NFTs help to create a free and fair economy by allowing consumers and companies to move real-world assets and services to the metaverse, a virtual, decentralized environment.

Because of the immutability and inherent transparency of the system, the potential of pumps and artificial value inflation with the basic law of supply and demand is limited. This is due to the scarcity and value of the NFT on the blockchain.

Individuals: This allows for the display of commodities and the usage of unique avatars across several platforms. These avatars are one-of-a-kind, and only one individual may buy them.

NFT avatars are virtual extensions of our real-life selves, enabling us to curate and develop our virtual selves in the metaverse with total autonomy and control.

Tradespersons: Artwork, gaming items, and stills or video from a live broadcast are just some of the digital outputs that may be "tokenized." In a virtual store, this may be shown and sold. Users may sell and purchase virtual locations in the metaverse.

Users may verify ownership of an object and construct virtual real estate as they see fit thanks to the underlying blockchain. They might even rent it out to supplement their income.

The digital real estate sector in the metaverse is exemplified by Decentraland, which recently hosted a virtual fashion show with Adidas in which works were auctioned as NFTs. Virtual real estate is particularly appealing to musicians and other artists since it allows them to perform and sell NFT tickets and merchandise online.

As noted earlier, the metaverse may be utilized for instruction through simulation, as described in prior chapters. If given the opportunity, Metaverse might easily aid conventional institutions in tackling the issue of remoteness.

Students who have finished a degree may be given an NFT by their institution, allowing employers to quickly verify an applicant's education. Apart from that, NFTs might be utilized to prevent fraud by marking certificates sent online for virtual seminars and workshops.

Game economy based on play-to-earn: Because customers add value to the system but get no reward; the gaming system is communist, using NFT will engage and empower blockchain game players. In order to battle better and tougher, gamers may purchase ammo and level up their characters while playing games.

After acquiring these ammunitions and upgrades, the builders retain ownership of the game. The internet is becoming more capitalist as a result of NFTs; you own what you generate or give to the internet, and your time, money, and effort are not squandered. To promote community and social relationships, use the following strategies: Holding certain NFTs may signal a user's acceptance of a community, similar to how owning a club's I.D. card indicates membership.

People who have comparable NFTs might build groups to share their stories and create content together. NFT avatars may be used as entry and exit tokens in the metaverse.

Non-Financial Transactions (NFTs) and Investing Alternatives

We discussed numerous cryptocurrencies and blockchain in depth in the last chapter. If you've been keeping up with recent tech headlines, you've probably heard about NFTs. News of multi-million-dollar auctions for digital assets has piqued the interest of both artists and collectors. NFTs, on the other hand, are a bit of a misnomer. What is their purpose, and how does it work? NFTs, their fundamental ideas, how they function, NFTs and blockchain, and other topics will be covered in this chapter. The foundations of non-fungible tokens, the technology behind them, and how they're utilized in daily life will be covered in this chapter. We'll also go over some of the abilities and information you'll need.

What is NFT, and what is its significance?

NFTs are one-of-a-kind assets that provide collectors and players ultimate ownership over their digital assets. Let's go through some fundamental vocabulary definitions first. To grasp what NFTs are and how they function, we'll need some background knowledge.

NFT

Non-fungible tokens (NFTs) are digital assets that represent a wide range of physical and intangible items, like valued sports cards, virtual real estate, and maybe even digital footwear. One of the most major benefits of owning a digital collectable over a physical collection, such as a Pokemon card or even a rare struck coin, is that each NFT has unique features that separate it from the others and can be readily verified. Because each item can be traced back to its original issuer, fake collectibles are useless to produce and disseminate.

A fungible asset, in economics, is money. It's disassembled into components that may be exchanged without losing or gaining value. Gold, bitcoins, and shares are all examples of fungible assets. On the other hand, non-fungible assets are one-of-a-kind objects such as houses, artworks, and trading cards. The original is still the original, even if it is replicated or photographed, and copies may not be worth as much. NFTs are digital data storage units that are kept on the blockchain. Each non-fungible token serves as an authentication certificate, confirming that a digital asset is one-of-a-kind and non-transferable. Because of cryptographic concepts that make the blockchain unique, an NFT can never be modified, changed, or stolen.

The Basics of NFT

NFTs, or non-fungible tokens, are online content pieces linked to the blockchain, a public database that supports cryptocurrencies like Bitcoin and Ethereum. Those commodities, unlike NFTs, are fungible, which means they may be changed or swapped for another of comparable value, akin to a dollar note. NFTs, on the other hand, are unique and non-interchangeable, meaning that no two NFTs are the same. Consider a set of limited-edition Jordans, rare coins, or Pokémon cards. NFTs, which come with a proof of authenticity, generate scarcity among otherwise eternally accessible goods. GIFs, photographs of tangible objects, tweets, virtual trade cards, and other digital artwork may all be purchased and sold with NFTs. Skins for video games, virtual real estate, and more are all available.

What is the mechanism behind NFTs?

Unlike other cryptocurrencies, NFTs can't be exchanged directly. Even whether they're from the same platform, game, or collection, no two NFTs are exactly same. Take their festival tickets into consideration. Each ticket contains information such as the buyer's name, the event's date, and the venue. Due to this information, it is unable to exchange festival tickets. The vast majority of NFT tokens were created using one of two Ethereum token standards (ERC-721 or ERC-1155), which are blueprints created by Ethereum that allow software teams to quickly deploy NFTs while also ensuring that they are interoperable with a wide range of platforms, including exchanges and wallet services like MetaMask and MyEtherWallet. To enable developers to construct and host NFTs utilizing respective blockchain networks, Eos, Neo, and Tron have created their own NFT token standards. Non-interoperable, indivisible, indestructible, and verifiable

NFTs are non-interoperable, indivisible, indestructible, and verifiable NFTs are non-interoperable, indivisible, indestructible, and verifiable NFTs are non-interoperable, indivisible, indestructible, It's also possible to buy and sell NFTs.

What are the best ways to get NFTs?

Every digital picture may theoretically be purchased as an NFT at any time. There are a few things to keep in mind before getting one, particularly if you're a rookie. You'll need to choose a marketplace to buy from, as well as a mobile currency to keep your cryptocurrency in and the cryptocurrency you'll need to complete the transaction. OpenSea, Nifty Gateway, Mintable, and Rarible are a few of the most well-known NFT markets.

How should NFTs be sold out?

Markets may also be used to buy NFTs, however the process varies per platform. Essentially, you'll sell your work on a marketplace and then use the supplied procedures to turn it into an NFT. You'll be able to provide details like a work description and a price proposal. NFTs are mostly bought using Ethereum, and they're often bought with ERC-20 tokens like WAX and Flow.

What Is an NFT and How Do I Make One?

The creation of an NFT is possible for everyone. All you'll need is a digital wallet, some Ethereum, and access to the NFT marketplace, where you can submit your work and transform it into an NFT or crypto art. If you're a budding digital artist, you may want to consider making NFTs for your projects. Fortunately, you can get started using a variety of platforms. In general, the procedure is straightforward, and the different platforms will guide you through the process. However, there are a few things to consider before getting started. A specialized blockchain is used to build and support NFTs. Non-fungible tokens are increasingly using the Ethereum network. To get started, you'll want a bitcoin wallet as well as cryptocurrency. The most widely used cryptocurrency at the moment is ether (ETH). You may create and sell digital assets via an NFT marketplace. The OpenSea platform, which is built on Ethereum, has a large following.

Blockchain and the NFT

Today, blockchain technology comes in a variety of flavors. Some blockchains were built to meet the demands of a small group of individuals with restricted network access. So, how do NFTs fit into the realm of blockchain technology? Remember, a blockchain is a piece of software that serves as a distributed ledger among nodes in a network. Its immutability distinguishes it from other online databases or trading platforms: we may exchange digital assets peer to peer, and no one can modify or delete those transactions unless a majority of the network agrees. When it comes to the Internet, this is a big plus.

NFT's Debut

While NFTs are still the "shiny new object" of the digital financial ecosystem, their usefulness and market value are yet unknown. To reach their full potential among general consumers, NFTs must be represented and provided in mid-market settings, not only in high-end, top-of-the-line options. The average consumer needs information, as well as the ability to search, compare, and shop. A buyer's journey begins with the discovery stage. Don't underestimate the influence of impulsive purchases. NFT markets will most likely become more specialized as a result of this. One of the first NFT markets, OpenSea, is exploding in popularity. In 2021, OpenSea trading volumes surged by more than 12,000 percent, with a record $150 million in NFT transactions in June alone. If that wasn't enough good news, their user base rose from 315 to 14,520 in only six months, pushing the firm to a $3 billion monthly NFT volume in August. All of this is great news for the NFT and the digital finance industry as a whole, but a niche marketplace can't take the sector ahead as rapidly as a globally renowned behemoth like Alibaba. That's why Alibaba's most recent statement is so intriguing. Alibaba Group Holding (BABA), a Chinese e-commerce powerhouse, created a new NFT marketplace earlier this month with the approval of the province government of Sichuan.

The marketplace was launched using Alibaba Auction, Alibaba's online auction platform. The scheme, branded "Blockchain Digital Copyrights & the Asset-Trade," enables authors, singers, and other artists to use blockchain technology to sell out the rights to their entire body of work. The NFTs will be issued by the Sichuan Blockchain Organization Copyright Committee's Fresh Copyright Blockchain platform. Despite its crackdown on private cryptocurrencies, China's government is enthused about blockchain technology. Alibaba can now sell NFTs thanks to them. It indicates that the NFT model has considerably more applications in China than only digital art, virtual game assets, and collectibles. They seem to understand the benefits of using NFTs to replace and automate obsolete processes like public registers (especially, in this instance, copyright registration) and applying the technology to property, patents, and other domains.

Smart Contracts are a kind of contract that uses artificial intelligence

NFTs are created using smart contracts that allocate ownership and regulate transferability. When someone creates or mints an NFT, they are executing code from smart contracts that are compliant with multiple standards, such as

ERC-721. The NFT is handled on the blockchain, which stores this data. Smart contracts have had a big influence on the general public in the form of Non-Fungible Tokens (NFTs). More than $2 billion was spent on NFTs in the first quarter of 2021, representing a 2,100% increase over the fourth quarter of 2020.

Asset (Digital)

A digital asset is simply anything that exists in digital form and can be utilised (duplicate, a right to copy, reproduce, and modify). Digital assets, for example, include documents, audio or video information, images, and other digital data.

Cryptocurrencies vs. NFTs

The distinction between cryptocurrencies and non-fungible tokens is critical. Despite the fact that they both use blockchain technology, knowing the key distinctions between them will help you grasp how NFTs work. The most significant difference is that cryptocurrencies are fungible. One Bitcoin may be exchanged for another, for example. You won't be able to accomplish this with an NFT, though. The term "non-fungible token" refers to a token that cannot be exchanged

one that is linked to a single digital asset and cannot be exchanged for another The main difference between the NFT and cryptocurrency is that, unlike cryptocurrency, NFTs are one-of-a-kind representations of real-world goods that cannot be traded. Because the value of cryptocurrencies does not depreciate, they can be traded for each other. Cryptocurrencies and NFTs, on the other hand, are decentralized and governed by their respective communities. Cryptocurrencies and NFTs can also be accessed through a digital public ledger, making all transactions transparent.

NFT vs. Bitcoin: What's the Difference?

While an NFT uses the same technology as a cryptocurrency such as Bitcoin, the two are otherwise unrelated. Bitcoins can be exchanged for one another and have the same value, just like one rupee is always worth another rupee and one Bitcoin is always worth another Bitcoin, regardless of price fluctuations compared to other similar currencies. Other materials are not as good as NFTs. Each NFT (virtual asset) has a digital signature that can't be replicated exactly because of the encoding.

The Advantages and Disadvantages of NFTs

Below are some potential advantages and disadvantages:

Advantages of NFTs

The following are some of the benefits of NFTs:

Security

NFTs can be traded safely and transparently. NFTs function as irreversible digital signatures, providing collectors with a high level of trust. This assurance also includes the art's long-term legacy. Although the blockchain protects digital works from censorship and physical degradation, they must still be stored with caution. People can also use blockchain technology to send large amounts of money around the world securely and in full view of the public. NFTs now ensure the legitimacy, uniqueness, and ownership of unique assets, in the same way that blockchain technology created a trust protocol that enabled the creation of digital currency.

Appreciation of Value

Physical valuables (such as art) have a long history of increasing in value, and digital art may be next.

Buyers and sellers will have more options.

When you buy and sell digital assets as NFTs, you have access to a much larger pool of buyers.

than before, both buyers and sellers

They hand over digital assets to artists.

An NFT enables content creators to demonstrate authenticity while also profiting from their digital asset. For the creators of widely shared memes, this could be a significant revenue stream.

They're one-of-a-kind and collector's items.

The thrill of owning a one-of-a-kind or extremely rare item is appealing to many people. NFTs add an extra layer of authenticity to collectible content, particularly digital goods.

They can't be altered.

Because they are blockchain-based, non-fungible tokens cannot be changed, deleted, or replaced. When proving the origin or authenticity of digital content, this is an important feature to have.

Composability

NFTs can be compared to interconnected Lego pieces, which is one of the most exciting aspects of them. This means that designers can create new NFTs based on previous NFTs' success. Because of its modular nature, any NFT project can be considered a component of a larger, interconnected ecosystem.

Smart Contracts are one example.

Another fascinating feature of blockchain technology is smart contracts. They can basically store instructions that are executed when certain criteria are met. As a result, if the NFT is sold in the future, an NFT with a smart contract could provide artists with a portion of the profit. Smart contracts, which are a series of coded commands incorporated into the blockchain, allow artists and producers to be paid in the future based on the use and resale of their work.

NFT drawbacks

NFTs have the following drawbacks:

They're inherently speculative.

The big question is whether NFTs are useful. Is it a good long-term investment or just a passing fad? It's a tough call. The only criterion for valuing NFTs right now is their emotional value.

It is possible to duplicate digital assets.

The presence of a digital object's NFT does not rule out the possibility of copies. GIFs and videos can be shared hundreds of times, and art can be copied and pasted. Because you own the NFT, you don't have control over the asset; it's only proof of ownership.

Costs for the Environment

The impact of blockchain-based cryptocurrencies like Ether and Bitcoin on the environment has gotten a lot of press. It takes a lot of computing power to enter records into a blockchain. Blockchain-based assets' long-term viability is a major concern.

It's possible that they'll be taken from you.

While the technology behind NFTs is extremely secure, many of the exchanges and platforms are not. As a result, several reports of NFTs being stolen as a result of cyber security breaches have emerged.

Reduced demand causes a drop in value.

Because most NFTs are immobile assets that do not generate income on their own, subjective indicators like buyer demand are used to determine their value. As a result, sky-high prices may not last forever, and NFTs may lose a significant amount of their value.

The Future of the Environment

Similarly to blockchain transactions, creating and selling NFTs consumes a significant amount of energy. Some scientists fear that an expanding NFT market will exacerbate the effects of a rapidly deteriorating environment.

Control isn't the same thing as ownership.

The possession of an original NFT does not imply control over its distribution or duplication across platforms. They only own the "original" and have no power to prevent "prints" from being made.

What Factors Affect NFT Success?

NFTs can be your best friend or worst enemy, depending on how you use them. NFT projects are as unpredictable as British weather on a sunny day, but there are patterns among the chaos, and if yours can tap into one of them, your project could be worth a million dollars by Christmas. In the world of digital art, it could also fail quietly.

NFTs and Celebrity

Obtaining the assistance of a celebrity, such as a basketball player, world champion footballer, or ice hockey player, is the most straightforward way to succeed with an NFT project. In sports settings, NFTs thrive. On the open market, you can buy and sell trading cards, Andre Agassi's Ponytail, ticket stubs, signed shirts, uniforms, and a bloodied sock. NFT rights are part of Messi's new PSG deal. Sorare, a football-themed NFC collector card, received $532 million in funding. Sorare has signed contracts with football superpowers Japan, the United States, Belgium, Liverpool, the Netherlands, and West Ham United, among others. Football is essentially a money-printing license. In essence, a license to print money is what NFTs are. It's a competitive match made in heaven, and you'll need to contact an agency if you want your NFT project to succeed.

Catch the NFT Zeitgeist by copying, imitating, and copying.

Because nothing is truly unique, copy it. Ride the tidal wave, ride the zeitgeist, bask in the light of a Twitter storm, and unleash your 10,000 NFT collection on the OpenSea to a chorus of missed opportunities and hope. The success of CryptoPunks has spawned a swarm of imitators who profit from pixelated avatars and animal stories. The CryptoPunks' basic ideals have been adopted by CyberKongz, Bored Ape Yacht Club, Pudgy Penguins, and a zoo of pretenders.

Create a high-performing team and a unique NFT project.

Appoint a motivating leader and assemble a talented team to create an outstanding NFT. Nothing on an Amstrad CPC should be made public. Even though we're in the midst of a gold rush, you need to inspire the NFT audience. High on your priority list should be great artwork, a sound business model, and equal sharing. Create a community, don't just ask for money, and reward your customers with extras like exclusive online interviews and discussions. You'll have to think outside of the box.

Why do NFT projects fall short of their goals?

The ability to think creatively is a valuable asset. For all NFT ventures that do not deliver something novel, engaging, or fascinating, breaking through the noise and ranking well on the OpenSea or generating Twitter engagement will become increasingly difficult. There are copyright issues, environmental consequences (whether NFTs are destroying the icecaps or not is irrelevant to the media and headlines), and the nature of the eco-crooked system. Scams, security issues, rug pulls, and mismanagement of funds and projects are all major concerns. The success of your NFT project may be jeopardized for one or more of these reasons. Nothing in the world of NFTs and Bitcoin is ever predictable, of course. What will define a success in the months and years ahead?

The great NFT project will change dramatically, just as the marketplace and North Korea's supreme commander are both unpredictable.

Using NFTs to Buy and Sell Things in the Metaverse

NFTs (non-fungible tokens) are a new type of virtual property that has fueled much of the Metaverse's growth. A non-tangible digital object, like a video, image, or in-game item, is represented by an NFT. Because the owners of NFTs are listed on the blockchain, they can be traded as a substitute for the digital assets they represent. During the pandemic, the NFT industry grew dramatically, with sales reaching $2.5 billion in the first half of 2021, up from $13.7 million the previous year. Some NFT collectors regard them as collectibles with intrinsic value based on cultural significance, while others regard them as commodities in which they speculate on price increases. "Everyday - The Very First 5000 Days," a digital-only artwork by US artist Mike Winkelmann, better known as Beeple, was sold for nearly $70 million at Christie's in March, making it the first such work to be auctioned by the major auction house. Despite the fact that several Metaverse sites provide free accounts, anyone purchasing or selling virtual goods on blockchain-based platforms should use cryptocurrency. Various blockchain-based services require

Ethereum-based crypto tokens to buy and sell virtual assets, such as The Sandbox's SAND and Decentraland's MANA. Users can trade NFT artworks or request tickets to a virtual show or concert in Decentraland. They may also be able to make money by selling land, which has seen a significant increase in value in recent years. Users on Roblox can earn money by charging other Roblox users for access to their games.